fast

thinking:
flying start

PEARSON EDUCATION LIMITED

Head Office:
Edinburgh Gate
Harlow CM20 2JE
Tel: +44 (0)1279 623623
Fax: +44 (0)1279 431059

London Office:
128 Long Acre
London WC2E 9AN
Tel: +44 (0)20 7447 2000
Fax: +44 (0)20 7240 5771
Website: www.business-minds.com

First published in Great Britain in 2001

The right of Ros Jay to be identified as Author
of this Work has been asserted by her in accordance
with the Copyright, Designs and Patents Act 1988.

ISBN 0 273 65308 3

British Library Cataloguing in Publication Data
A CIP catalogue record for this book can be obtained from the British Library

10 9 8 7 6 5 4 3 2 1

Typeset by Pantek Arts Ltd, Maidstone, Kent.
Printed and bound in Great Britain by Ashford Colour Press, Hampshire

The Publishers' policy is to use paper manufactured from sustainable forests.

fast
thinking:
flying start

- ▶ **have first day confidence**
- ▶ **know the right people**
- ▶ **set off with style**

by Ros Jay

contents

introduction

Congratulations on your new job! Feeling nervous? Starting a new job is exciting, but it can be nerve-wracking too. What if you make a fool of yourself? What if you can't do the job? What if you don't get on with anyone? What if you fail to make your mark on the organization? What if you make a bad impression?

These are typical fears that we all have when we start a new job, whether it's a move within the company or a move to a completely new organization. And you've got to get it right first time. It's no good getting off on the wrong foot and thinking you can have another go next week. This is crunch time. No wonder you're nervous.

But you needn't be. You've come to the right place. This book contains everything you need to know to get off to a flying start in the first two or three days (with the modern speed of work, that's all the time you'll have before you get stuck deep into the job). But that's all you need. This book will take you through all the different aspects of getting started in your new role – from getting to know the people to establishing your objective –

regardless of whether your new employers also give you an induction course of their own.

You haven't got long. Maybe you start the job tomorrow morning. In any case, within a few days you'll be swamped with work. So you'll have to move fast to learn all you need to while you've still got the time. You need:

 tips for finding your feet fast

 shortcuts for learning what you need to know

 checklists to make sure you haven't missed anything

… all put together clearly and simply. And short enough to read fast, of course.

Well, you got it. Just follow the guidelines here and you'll make a stunning impression, and set yourself up to do a terrific job too. And if you're launching yourself into one of those jobs where you have hardly any time to settle in, you'll find a section at the back of the book on how to get off to a flying start in half a day. In fact, there's a section on how to make the best possible start in as little as an hour. So if you've got several days, you really are basking in luxury.

This book contains everything you need to know to get off to a flying start in the first two or three days

This book will take you through the six key areas you need to have covered when you start your new job:

1 To begin with, you need to get the practicalities – from loos to lunch breaks – sorted out, along with finding out everyone's names. And then there are the unspoken rules, philosophy and systems that you need to get to grips with.

2 You need some quick tips now on how to create a good first impression. This will make your job much easier when you get down to work.

3 Next, you need to find out exactly what your job is: your objective. That will inform everything else you do. And you need to establish the parameters of your job: what exactly your responsibilities are, what resources you have at your disposal, and so on. This means a meeting with your boss.

4 Now it's time to check out the history of your job and your department. You need to know precisely what you're taking over – the good bits and the bad bits.

5 You won't get far with your new job unless you know all about the people you're working with, from their talents to the internal politics. So that's your next task – getting to know your colleagues and team members.

6 Finally, once you've established what the job is all about, you need to assess your own ability to do it so that you can identify any weaknesses and remedy them before anyone else spots them. And, of course, you need to recognize where your strengths will come into play. You need to formulate an outline plan for your time in this job.

fast thinking gambles

This book is all about how to hit the ground running in your new job. You are likely to find yourself immersed in paperwork and meetings, budgets and special events within a few days, and you need to get through the essential background work of introducing yourself to the organization – and vice versa – as fast as possible.

In an ideal world (which you probably don't inhabit), you would spend about a fortnight settling into your new role before you started to schedule your time as though you were now fully integrated into the job. This is because when you induct yourself fast, there is always an element of gamble involved. Even if you have no choice in the matter, it's worth knowing the risks you take:

- There's a lot to learn, and inevitably the faster you work through it, the more chance there is that at least something will get missed. If it does, you just have to hope it's something minor and not critical.

- You've got to get to know your team members, and they all have to get used to you too. The more time you and your team have to size each other up before you get stuck into the work together, the better chance you all have of getting on and not rubbing each other up the wrong way.

- The subtle, unspoken things – secrets, even – are the ones that are most likely to get missed in the rush, and they are often the most important. Maybe no one's telling you that the organization will be in huge trouble if the press find out about the damning safety report – and as PR manager, you really need to know. Or perhaps your department's dreadful figures for last year are about to be announced and you'll have to sort out the mess without any warning – unless you've found out about it ahead of time.

With the help of this book, fast thinking should get you where you need to be in a couple of days rather than a couple of weeks, and no one but you will be able to tell the difference. But it's worth taking longer if you possibly can next time you start a new job – in a few months when you get promoted up the organization.

1 learning the ropes

It's nine o'clock in the morning, and you've just walked in on your first day in the new job. You've given your name to the receptionist, and your boss is on their way to meet you and take you to your desk. What are your immediate priorities?

Even without a formal induction process, your boss – or someone – is bound at least to show you where to hang your coat, where the loos are, and to give you any security codes you need in order to reach your office. Then they will, no doubt, whisk you round the part of the building you'll be spending most time in, and rush you through a whirl of introductions: 'This is Gabby; she's one of your sales assistants. And this is Mike, who handles several of the key accounts. Where's Doug? Doug seems to have popped out for a moment – well, you'll meet him later; anyway, he looks after the key accounts with Mike. And here's Ellen …'

With the best will in the world, people tend to dispense information faster than you can take it in. And you can find yourself being rushed – albeit kindly – to the point where you retain so little information you might as well have skipped this bit of the induction altogether.

SET YOUR OWN PACE

You can't afford to waste time being bombarded with information you can't absorb. It's far more time efficient in the long run to take a little longer but to end up remembering it all. So you need to set the pace yourself, politely but firmly, and find ways to help the information sink in. You can do this directly, simply by saying, 'I'm not sure I can take everything in at this speed. Can we slow down a little?' But there are also indirect ways of making the process more useful.

thinking smart

GET IT DOWN

Have a pen and a small notebook with you. Write down anything you can that you think you might forget, from the time the cafeteria opens to the security number to get through the doors. Once it's written down, it can't be forgotten and it's one less thing to have to retain in your head.

People

If you are swept through your department – and probably those other departments you'll be working closest with – with barely time to say more than 'Hi! Nice to meet you,' 'Hello,' and 'I'll catch up with you later,' you'll be lucky if you remember anyone's name or what they actually do. You may not even remember who is working under you and who is senior to you.

So resist the high-speed introductions firmly. As soon as you are told, 'This is Gabby; she's one of your sales assistants,' get in there fast with a question to Gabby before you can be hurried on to the next person. A question instantly sets up a conversation, which Gabby will join in with, and your guide will be too polite to interrupt.

You can ask just about anything, so long as it is an open question. In other words, a question to which Gabby has to give more than a one-word answer. For example:

▶ **What exactly does your job entail?**

▶ **How do you manage to keep your desk so amazingly tidy?**

▶ **Was it you I saw getting out of that Frog-eyed Sprite in the car park?**

MEMORY BOOST

It is far easier to remember someone's name if you say it out loud. So as soon as you're introduced to anyone, repeat their name: 'Hi, Gabby. How are you?' Don't worry if it seems stilted: it won't sound it. And anyway, everyone knows you've got a lot of names to remember, and they'll appreciate the fact that you're bothering to try to learn them.

So long as the question is polite and friendly, its content doesn't matter much. You're not asking because you need the information. You're asking because a 15- to 30-second conversation with someone will do far more to imprint them on your memory than a rushed 'good to meet you' and on to the next person. Not only that, but having a brief conversation with each person slows the whole process down to a manageable speed, where you have a chance to take in the information you really need (that the name of the sales assistant who sits over by the window is Gabby).

Places

When it comes to finding your way around places, there's no substitute for navigating your own way around. So, if your guide is taking you there and back again, ask to be allowed to find your own way back with them at your shoulder to tell you if you go wrong. If you're on a round trip, ask if they'll accompany you on a repeat journey with you navigating to see if you can do it. If they can't, take someone else with you or simply go on your own and see what happens. You've got to do it some time, and the sooner you make mistakes, the sooner you'll learn.

Systems

At this stage, systems are going to be fairly practical and straightforward. No one is likely to launch into what your department does with each of its triplicate petty cash forms for another day or two. But it is important to remember the systems you're told, because even as a newcomer you can make a fool of yourself if you're found queueing in the shop-floor workers' queue instead of the managers' queue at the canteen.

Again, the best way to remember anything is by doing it. So, ask to punch the security code into the keypad yourself, or go and sit at the right canteen table for a moment. By taking a little longer, you'll imprint the memory of what to do far more strongly.

As soon as you have time to sit down on your own for five minutes, write down everything you think you might forget. This might be a reminder of how to put names to faces, or a note of things to remember about people. If you meet 50 people today, and on Friday you still remember that Gabby is the one who drives the Frog-eyed Sprite, she'll be impressed and flattered. So jot down anything worth remembering about the people you've met.

You may also want to note down details of any systems you've been introduced to, such as how reception should be notified when visitors are expected, or how to find the fire escape where you're allowed to go for a smoke.

 thinking smart

PLAYING SAFE

Don't write down anything uncomplimentary about the people you'll be working with, just in case your notebook falls into the wrong hands. If your team members find notes such as 'Gabby – talks too much' or 'Mike – fat one with b.o.' you may find your popularity falling off fast.

The best way to remember anything is by doing it

UNSPOKEN RULES

Every organization has unspoken rules to learn, as well as the ones you'll be told about. Perversely, these unspoken rules are almost always more important to the people around you. Here are a few examples, but remember that they will vary widely from one organization to the next:

- ▶ Senior managers are addressed by title and surname, not forename.

- ▶ People always sit with their own teams in the cafeteria.

- ▶ Managers don't go into the rest room.

- ▶ Memos are always sent by email rather than hard copy.

- ▶ Managers always work through lunch.

- ▶ No one stays later than 6 o'clock in the evening.

- ▶ People work hard, with no gossiping round the coffee machine or over the photocopier.

- ▶ The manager treats the department to cream cakes every Friday morning.

All organizations are full of unwritten rules of this kind. The reason you won't be told about these rules is that everyone is so used to them that they take them for granted – it's only when you break them that your team members will notice that you just called the marketing director Peter, or that you left the building for an hour at lunch time.

It's an alarming fact that much of what determines whether you fit into your new job is your ability to slot into the company culture. Sure, your performance will count, but if the rest of the crowd feel that you're not 'one of them', you're far less likely to succeed. Some research claims that as many as 90 per cent of sackings are due to failure to fit into the culture. So, listening and watching to pick up on the signs that tell you what's expected of you is a vital skill. You'll find that much of the advice in the rest of this book is also geared to helping you get in tune with the corporate culture.

The only way to learn these rules is by looking out for them, and asking questions whenever you suspect an unspoken rule applies. It is sometimes inappropriate to ask directly, since people have a strange aversion to discussing certain rules directly, but you can always find a way around the problem. For example, you may start to get the impression that all budget decisions seem to go through the administration director as well as the finance director. If you ask why, you may meet with an uncomfortable silence (perhaps the reason is that the admin director used to be the finance director's boss and, despite promotion to an equal position, the finance director is still in the admin director's pocket). Don't try to find out all the details straight away – just stick to the basics: 'Am I right in thinking that budget decisions should be referred to the admin director as well as the finance director?' Once you've established the facts, you're not going to put your foot in it. Sooner or later, you'll learn the real reason.

Some of the more simple unspoken rules, such as how to address senior colleagues, will start becoming apparent from your first day. So be on the lookout for them, and ask for clarification if you feel you need to.

FIRST-DAY CHECKLIST

Before we finish this chapter, it's worth giving you a quick checklist of the practical things you can expect to cover, learn or be allocated in your first few hours (not all of them will apply to every job, of course). You can run through the list at the end of the day and make sure nothing important has been missed out.

- ▶ **Working hours (the real ones, which may not be exactly what it says on your contract).**

- ▶ **Lunchtimes and arrangements (eat in or out, or bring sandwiches?)**

- ▶ **Security codes and keys.**

- (▶) Computer password and email address.
- (▶) Direct phone number.
- (▶) Business cards.
- (▶) Check you are conversant with the computer software (or make arrangements to learn it fast).
- (▶) Location of photocopier, fax machine, key personnel and meeting rooms, loos, canteen.
- (▶) Location of personnel files, departmental budget, minutes of meetings.
- (▶) Locker, or at least a place to hang your coat.
- (▶) Salary arrangements – do you need to pass on your bank account details?

(▶) for later...

One of the best ways to get a feel for the organization and immerse yourself into its philosophy – as well as picking up many of the unspoken rules – is by reading about it. So get hold of copies of company newsletters (including back copies), the annual report, press releases and press cuttings, sales literature and anything else you can lay your hands on.

If you're reading this ahead of starting your new job, don't wait until you get there. Phone up now and ask them to send you all the material they can to give you a feel for the place.

2 first impressions

We all know that stuff about never getting a second chance to make a first impression. And it's all true. As you're being rushed around the offices on your whirlwind tour, your new colleagues are getting their first chance to form an opinion of you. After you've left each room, the people in it will be saying to each other, 'What did you think?' I'm not trying to make you paranoid here – they really are all talking about you.

But you needn't worry. All you have to do is to make a *good* impression, and they will be saying just what you'd like them to. And once formed, a first impression is hard (though not impossible) to break. So you give yourself a flying start if those first few meetings with the people who matter – your team, your colleagues, your bosses – leave them feeling pleased you've joined the company.

So the 64 million dollar question is: how do you make a good impression from the start? Well, there are plenty of things you can do – none of them difficult – to make sure people decide from the off that you are likeable, trustworthy and talented.

THINK ABOUT YOUR APPEARANCE

This is really pretty straightforward. Keep your hair, teeth and nails clean and all that stuff. The most important thing is to fit in with everyone else. If you turn up in a smart suit when everyone else is wearing jeans and T-shirts, they will instinctively feel you're not one of them. Equally, if you turn up in a casual outfit and find all your colleagues dressed in tailored suits, you're not going to find it easy to slot into the company culture.

thinking smart

NEARLY NEW IS BETTER THAN BRAND NEW
Your first day in a new job is not the time to wear a new outfit, appropriate though it may seem. There are few worse times to find out that your new shoes are pinching and giving you blisters, or that your new top keeps riding up under your skirt, or that the collar on the shirt you bought yesterday is too tight. If you really want to wear new clothes – and for some people it is a psychological boost – at least wear them at home for an evening first to break them in.

There's only one sure-fire answer to this dilemma: find out in advance what everyone wears at your new workplace. Think back to your interview. What was the interviewer wearing? Did you get a chance to see anyone else and, if so, what sort of clothes were they wearing?

If this line of thought doesn't help much, do you know anyone who works at the organization already whom you could call? If not, call the person who interviewed you, or their secretary. It's a perfectly reasonable question, so you've nothing to feel uncomfortable about. Just say, 'I want to make sure I fit in, so could you give me an idea of the dress code in the company?'

BE ENERGETIC

One of the most vital and attractive characteristics – especially for a manager – is energy. You must have met people with limp handshakes who always sound wishy-washy and half asleep. Don't be one of them. You don't have to overpower people; simply come across from the start as someone with a positive attitude and the energy to carry your ideas through.

▶ **Don't speak too softly.**

▶ **Be ready with a firm handshake.**

- (▶) Smile broadly when you meet people.
- (▶) Make eye contact.
- (▶) Say hello to people readily and with enthusiasm.
- (▶) Be ready to speak confidently without always waiting to be called on to speak – you can be the first to say hello.
- (▶) Sound interested in what you're saying, and in what other people say to you.
- (▶) Move and speak at an upbeat pace (without rushing).

You don't have to turn yourself into something you're not – that never works – but we all have a range of behaviours we can call on, and the trick is to know which aspects of yourself to bring to the fore.

thinking smart

CALL ON YOUR EXPERIENCE

Think about people you know who always come across as energetic, and think about what it is they do that makes them seem so full of energy. Is it their tone of voice, their movements, their manner, their speed? And try the reverse, too. What makes low-energy people come across in this way?

BE LIKEABLE

You hear all sorts of theories about what makes a good manager, some more convincing than others. But one quality that is essential in a top-class manager is likeability. When people like you, they want to work hard for you. The whole task of motivating your team is vastly easier and more effective if they like you.

So how do you get people to like you? It's pretty simple really. You know what qualities make people popular and which don't. But here's a run-down of the most important:

▶ Be a good listener.

▶ Take a genuine interest in other people.

▶ Be fair (and be seen to be fair).

▶ Care about the people who work for you.

▶ Don't set yourself above the rest of the team (take your turn at making the coffee).

▶ Don't gossip about anyone in your team behind their backs.

▶ Make time for people when they need to talk to you.

▶ If you have a strong sense of humour, that's great; but don't use sarcasm or direct humour against anyone you work with.

▶ Don't be arrogant or pompous.

If you follow these guidelines – which anyone should be able to do regardless of their natural personality – your new colleagues will undoubtedly like you. You don't have to give in to them, sidestep necessary confrontations, or overlook poor performance. If you are liked, you will be respected even more for dealing fairly and squarely with uncomfortable situations when it is clearly necessary.

INSPIRE TRUST

There is a very simple formula for appearing trustworthy, and that is to be open and honest. If you are honest it will show, and people will recognize that you can be trusted to deal with them fairly and to be straight with them. You need to be open as well, so people can see that you're not the type to keep secrets, hold back important information, or be two-faced.

Your new team members will be looking for this quality in their new manager. They need to know that you will be a boss they can trust. You can demonstrate your honesty by being open about answering any questions they have, and by being open about your personal life too. That doesn't mean you have to bare your soul to them, but don't be secretive. Be comfortable mentioning where you went on holiday, or that you have a sister in Edinburgh, or how passionate you are about music.

CONVINCE THEM YOU'VE GOT TALENT

The key here is to show, not tell. If you go round bragging about how successful you were in your last job, or what an instinct you have for problem solving, you'll simply turn people off. They won't think, 'Wow, he must be good!' or 'She's just what we need round here.' They will actually think, 'What an arrogant little sh**.' You'll have blown all the hard work you put into being likeable.

And worse, it won't even work. If people don't like you, they won't want it to be true. So they won't believe it. 'I bet it wasn't really like that at all,' they'll whisper to each other.

So don't tell them. Show them. Remain modest and don't shout about past achievements, but act smart and they'll soon be saying to each other, 'That was a really neat idea – why has nobody thought of that before?' They will admire your achievements and your modesty. And they'll wonder what else you're capable of.

Don't get so hung up about making a good first impression that you end up too nervous. Remind

READY ... AIM ... FIRE!

When you first arrive in a new job, do a lot more listening than talking. At those early meetings, don't say too much until you have something to say that you know is really smart. Then come out with it (without sounding as if you know you're being smart). This will be the first big impression you've made regarding your talent – so make it a good one. After that, it would take an awful lot of really pathetic ideas to shake everyone's view that you may not say much, but what you *do* say is worth listening to.

yourself that you obviously got it right at the interview or you'd never have got the job. So feel confident without being cocky, and with a little bit of conscious effort along the lines we've just covered, it should all flow naturally.

for later ...

Make sure that these initial impressions remain part of your everyday behaviour. No one will be fooled for long if the mask slips after the first couple of weeks. So make sure it's no mask. Work on being consistently energetic, likeable, trustworthy and talented ... and you'll have the makings of a first-class manager.

If you go round bragging about how successful you were in your last job, you'll simply turn people off

3 meeting the boss

Once you've said hello to everyone and taken your coat off, it's time to crack on with the job. And the first thing you need to do is to have a meeting with your boss. With some luck, your boss will have set aside the first part of the morning for you anyway, so this is your best chance to have the meeting you want, as well as covering anything they want to discuss (which may well overlap).

But even if this meeting isn't already scheduled, you must have it. You may need to be assertive and explain to your boss that you don't feel you can really get your teeth into this job until you've covered certain topics together. Their input is sufficiently important (a bit of subtle flattery always helps, especially when it's true) that this meeting needs to come first. You shouldn't have too much trouble getting half an hour or so of their time on your first morning.

So, now you have your boss to yourself, what

PHONE AHEAD

If it isn't already too late, give your new boss a ring a few days before you start your job to schedule in a meeting shortly after you arrive.

are you going to talk to them about? There are five key questions you must have the answers to before you can get on with the job:

1 What is your objective?
2 What is expected of you?
3 Why did you get the job?
4 What resources do you have?
5 What authority do you have?

WHAT IS YOUR OBJECTIVE?

Excuse me? Objective? What's this all about? What are we doing setting objectives before we've even found out what the job entails?

Well, we're not setting an objective for a particular project; we're setting the objective for your job. What are you here for? You can't do your job properly unless you know exactly what job you are there to do. But your objective isn't simply 'to

GET IT IN WRITING

In a professional, up-together organization, your objective should appear on your job description. If you're lucky, it will be there already for you, in which case you may simply want to talk it through with your boss. If it isn't on your job description, ask for it to be added.

run the department' – that isn't particularly helpful at all. And an objective should, above all, be helpful.

Your objective will also be the core objective of your department, and if none of you knows what it is, you're going to be floundering. So decide what you think it is and ask your boss to confirm it – or correct it – for you. Your objective clearly depends on your job, but here are a few examples:

Post	Possible objective
Sales manager	To increase profits
Accounts manager	To ensure accurate, helpful billing and payment systems
Production manager	To improve productivity
PR manager	To increase positive public awareness
Distribution manager	To ensure fast, high-quality distribution at minimum cost
Marketing manager	To build customer loyalty and attract new customers

As you can see, the objective may not always be obvious. As a new marketing manager, you might think that your objective is to build customer loyalty while your boss might consider that it is to attract new customers. Maybe it's both – a joint objective. But if you don't discuss it with your boss, you could be in big trouble in six months' time when hardly any new customers have been acquired … while you were expecting to be congratulated on increasing customer retention.

Your objective needs to be clear so that you can keep an eye on it permanently. It is your way of making sure you and your team don't get bogged down in day-to-day work without ever really achieving anything worthwhile (you've seen it happen to other people often enough). Once you have a clear objective, you can ensure that the bulk of the work that gets done in your department is directed at meeting it.

WHAT IS EXPECTED OF YOU?

Your objective is your core aim – you can check any task against it to see that it meets your objective. This way you can ensure that you don't get sidetracked and waste time on unimportant activities (since you certainly don't have time to fritter). But your objective doesn't give you any detail. It tells you where you're headed, but it doesn't tell you how fast to get there, or what to bring with you. You need more specific guidance.

What you really need to know – and only your boss can tell you – is what you are expected to achieve in the job. Maybe you're the new production manager and your objective is to increase productivity. But by how much? If it goes up by 2 per cent in the next year, will you think you've done well? And will your boss think you've failed?

So ask your boss the two key questions:

▸ **What am I expected to achieve in the next three months/six months/year?**

▸ **How will I know if I've failed in my job after the next three months/six months/year?**

thinking smart

DO YOUR HOMEWORK

Before you meet your boss – even before you start the job – it's worth working out your own suggested answers to the questions of what your objective is, and what is expected of you. A really smart boss will have no trouble at all answering these questions (indeed they will be pleased to hear you ask them), but a less on-the-ball boss may need some prompting. It is easier for them to correct your proposal than to create their own out of thin air.

Ask for specific figures or targets, and don't settle for anything vague that you can't work to, such as 'Well, we'd like to see productivity go up, of course.' Insist – politely – on concrete targets. Without them, you can't be expected to do your job properly.

WHY DID YOU GET THE JOB?

When you applied for this job, you were probably not the only applicant. Some of the others may have been rubbish, but at least some of them will have been good – maybe all of them were. And yet you were the one they chose. Why?

You must have had some qualities, experience or skills that particularly attracted your new employers. Something that made them think you would be more valuable to them than any of those other promising candidates. Something they really needed bringing to this job.

Wouldn't it be helpful to know what it is? If they were particularly looking for someone who was a good diplomat after all the problems the last manager caused, or they were especially impressed with your experience of dealing with the press because improving press relations is high on their agenda, you want to know about it.

What you really need to know – and only your boss can tell you – is what you are expected to achieve in the job

The answer to this question is going to give you a big clue as to where senior management's priorities lie when it comes to your new department, so make sure you ask it. Don't be shy: it's a perfectly reasonable – not to say intelligent – question. 'What was it that made you decide to offer the job to me? What in particular were you expecting I could bring to the job?'

WHAT RESOURCES DO YOU HAVE?

You wouldn't decide to bake a cake without knowing first what ingredients you had, and you can't start doing a job until you know what resources you have at your disposal. So ask your boss for:

- ▶ **a copy of the current budget for your department**
- ▶ **details of what staff you have and for what hours (if Gabby disappears every Friday for training, then you need to know about it)**
- ▶ **information about any other staff you can call on – can you bring in outsiders or call on staff from other departments for particular events? If you run big sales presentations, can you use in-house catering staff to provide coffees and lunches for your customers?**
- ▶ **information on access to other parts of the building, such as the conference hall or meeting rooms. Do you have to book? Do you take priority? What's the system?**

Depending on your job, there are all sorts of other resources you might need to find out about, such as:

- ▶ **time allocated to you on certain equipment**
- ▶ **use of company vehicles**
- ▶ **use of the in-house newsletter to post notices or information**

… and so on. So make sure your boss tells you exactly what tools you are being given to do the job.

WHAT AUTHORITY DO YOU HAVE?

This question is very much the partner of the previous one. As well as knowing what tools you have, you need to know how freely you are allowed

II thinking smart

PERSONAL AUTHORITY

As with resources, many areas of authority will be specific to your job. For example, as PR manager, can you authorize any press release to be sent out yourself, or do certain releases have to be approved by someone else first? As distribution manager, do you handle crises such as postal strikes yourself, or do you have to refer such decisions to your boss?

You wouldn't decide to bake a cake without knowing first what ingredients you had, and you can't start doing a job until you know what resources you have to use them. What decisions are you authorized to take yourself, and which do you have to refer up the line?

The kinds of areas that you'll need to know about are:

▶ **Staff** – can you hire and fire them?

▶ **Expenditure** – what can you authorize yourself?

▶ **Budget** – how much room for manoeuvre do you have within your overall budget before having to check back with your boss or finance department?

▶ **Other departments** – for example, do you have authority to borrow catering staff for specific events (by arrangement, obviously), or can the catering manager refuse?

▶ **Overtime** – can you authorize it yourself so long as you stay within budget?

Again, without this information you cannot either plan or execute your job. So pin your boss down to give you the answers to these questions so that you can meet your objective successfully.

▶ for later...

Once you have been in the job for a week, it will be time to start planning for your first success (if you don't make your mark soon, you'll get so bogged down in everyday work it may never happen). This plan should be ready to put into action at the end of your first fortnight. You might plan to win a major contract, set and meet a new sales target, solve a long-standing problem left behind by your predecessor, organize a major event, or maybe streamline a system that will lead to cost savings or increased productivity. Only you can decide what your big success will be, but you will need the answers to the questions we've just covered to choose a suitable plan.

Whatever plan you choose, it should:

- ▶ meet the objective for your job
- ▶ fulfil what is expected of you – or work towards it
- ▶ utilize the strengths for which you were appointed
- ▶ use resources that you are in a position to allocate
- ▶ fall within your sphere of authority.

So you see, you need the answers to these questions to be able to make your mark early on.

There's one other criterion your first success should fulfil: it shouldn't take too long to come to fruition. You can also, by all means, embark on long-term plans that will show big profit increases, cost savings, PR advantage or productivity boosts in two or three years' time. But for your first success, you need to find a project or challenge that will demonstrate your talents within your first three months or so.

4 taking stock

So, what have you let yourself in for? Is this a thriving, successful department? Or is it already way over budget for this year, with plummeting profits and three unfair dismissal claims pending? Is team morale high, or are your staff already queueing up outside your door to hand in their letters of resignation?

Your next task is to find out what you can about the job and the department you've just taken on. Clearly this is a process that will take time, but since time is a commodity in very short supply at the moment, you can kick-start the process with an intensive research session that will get you a lot of information in the shortest possible time.

You will learn a lot of what you need to know when you talk to your team, but you need to have some level of forewarning before you sit down with them formally. Otherwise you will have no idea what to expect, or what topics they might try to duck or cover up.

CHECKING IN

Your top priority for the first few days in your new job (and indeed all your subsequent time in it) is your team. Learning the background to the job may be more urgent at the moment, but you should be seen to spend time with your team from the start. So, after you've finished your meeting with your boss, have a cup of coffee with your team and a few minutes of social chat before you start ploughing through files. And if this process takes a long time, take regular breaks to talk to your team – even start on the individual team interviews (covered in the next chapter) in between bouts of research.

Your next task is to find out what you can about the job and the department you've just taken on

THE FILES

A lot of the information you need to unearth will already be close to hand. You need to root out the most important files and have a good look through them. If there's a lot to go through, have a quick look now to pick up anything vital (you've got a lot of other things to get through today, too), and take the files home for a more thorough study later. But as you'll see, you need to have garnered at least some of this information in order to get the most from your team interviews, so this has to come first – even if only the fast thinking version.

DO IT YOURSELF

As you go through the files, you may want to mark certain pages or make notes. Often, your new desk isn't equipped with the basics when you first arrive, so take a supply of essentials into work with you on your first day:

- pens
- paper
- highlighter pens
- post-it notes

... and anything else you think you're likely to need. That way, you won't have to hang around waiting for stationery supplies.

The main paperwork you need to check out is the personnel files, key project files, customer/supplier relationship files and the budget.

Personnel files

As we'll see in the next chapter, one of your first tasks is to interview all the members of your team individually. But you need to have looked through their personnel files first, so you know what you're dealing with. This will tell you a great deal about their skills, experience, strengths and weaknesses.

Key project files

You haven't got time right now to memorize every detail of every project your department has been involved in, but you must know about the most important ones. So dig out the files on all the major current projects and initiatives, and go through them to give yourself a good working knowledge of what's going on. You may be asked to make an important and urgent decision on one of these projects in the next few days, so you'd better know the background. (You'll find a page at the back of the book to make your own notes about key projects.)

If you find that there are clear problems with any of your key projects, make a note to discuss them with your team members when you talk to them individually. You may learn all sorts of useful things that you'd never have uncovered if you hadn't known which questions to ask. So make notes of what you want to know, such as, 'Why did we handle the late delivery problems this way?' or 'Why are Jones & Co. so reluctant to sign up to this deal?'

Customer/supplier relationship files

You will have key customers and suppliers, whatever your department's role. If you don't deal with outside organizations, you must have internal customers and suppliers. So once again, go through the key files and find out which relationships are good and which are in trouble, and why. Note down questions to ask your team (or anyone else), such as, 'What's the history of the relationship between our department and accounts?' or 'Why are we dealing with AB&C when they don't seem to be giving us the kind of discounts I'd expect?'

Budget

It is essential that you find out what your existing budget is, and whether you are meeting it or not. It may be that you are arriving in a department that is already critically over budget. If so, you need to find out fast, and find out why. Again, you can question your team members or your boss: 'Why are we so over budget on overtime?'

thinking smart

RULE YOUR DEPARTMENT

When William the Conqueror won the English throne, he soon realized that it was impossible to rule a kingdom if you didn't know what was in it. So he commissioned a huge research exercise to find out exactly what he owned and what revenues he could expect. He called it the *Domesday Book*. Nothing's changed – if you want to run your department effectively, you must find out everything about it first.

44

Get acquainted with your budget as quickly as you can, and find out how soon you will be expected to put in your proposal for the next budget. (If you're not used to dealing with budgets, take a look at *Fast Thinking: Budget*.)

YOUR PREDECESSOR

Assuming this isn't a new post you're filling, someone else was doing this job until recently. Even if it is a new post, most of the work may have been allocated to someone else. And that someone else could save you an awful lot of valuable time by telling you most of what you really need to know.

So, one of your most important tasks is to get hold of your predecessor and pick their brains. Your boss or your boss's secretary should be more than happy to tell you where to contact them. Of course, your predecessor might actually be your boss, or they might still be in the organization. But even if they're not, that's fine too. Your only problem is if they left under a cloud, or were moved reluctantly elsewhere in the organization. Assuming this isn't the case, most people will be more than happy to give help and advice to a grateful listener.

So what should you ask your predecessor, once you've made contact with them? If you've already

It is essential that you find out what your existing budget is, and whether you are meeting it or not

CATCH THEM EARLY

Your introduction to this new job is hurried and busy enough. So if you can, talk to your predecessor *before* you start the job. Get their phone number and arrange to buy them a drink or at least talk on the phone, and get all the information you can out of them. If they're willing, get permission to call them if you have problems once you've started in the job. Don't – obviously – ask them how to do the job, but one or two calls over the first few weeks to ask what went wrong with the MPQ contract last year, or what the background is to the rivalry between your department and marketing, is perfectly in order.

looked through the files, that will give you a lot of clues. But whether or not you have, here are some key questions to ask:

- ▶ **What did you find were the strengths of your team?**

- ▶ **And what did you feel were their weaknesses?**

- ▶ **Did you run into any particular problems during your time in the department?**

- ▶ **How did you deal with them?**

- ▶ **Are there any difficult dynamics within the team?**

- ▶ **Did you encounter problems with other departments in the organization?**

- ▶ **Did you have any specific problems with the departmental budget?**
- ▶ **Are there any organizational secrets I ought to know about?**

Don't forget that your predecessor has an ego, and won't be half so helpful if there's any implication from you that they weren't doing a good job. So if they went way over budget, don't say, 'Blimey, you know how to blow a budget, don't you? Where did you go wrong there, then?' Far better to phrase it diplomatically: 'It looks as if you weren't given nearly enough overall budget to play with. What were your biggest problems with it?'

SKELETONS IN THE CLOSET

Not all organizations have worrying secrets, but many do. And it may turn out that you have just started working for one of them. They may be large or small skeletons; either way you need to be on the lookout for them. It is unlikely that you will be told about them officially – at least not in your first few days – so you need to find out about them in other ways.

So what sort of skeletons are we talking about here? Well, anything that could make your job particularly difficult or even unsafe.

Serious interpersonal or interdepartmental warfare

This can be a big problem for a manager. If the despatch department are traditionally at loggerheads with your sales department, you want to know about it sooner rather than later. Healthy competition is one thing, but unpleasantness, back-biting and having your authority or success deliberately undermined are a different matter. The chances are that your team will let you know about this, but it doesn't hurt to ask anyone – from your boss to the canteen staff – to tell you if this is a happy organization or a bitchy one.

Interpersonal problems in your team can also be very hard to deal with, especially when you barely know the people involved. At this stage, the most important thing is to identify the problem correctly. If you sense trouble, have a quiet word with your boss. Explain that you feel things aren't right, and ask what the problem is. Then you can do something about resolving it. (If you need help resolving such problems, try *Fast Thinking: Difficult People*.)

Business or financial problems

Maybe your new employer is about to go bust. Or perhaps half the directors are about to be investigated for fraud. Maybe you're about to be taken over, or perhaps your department's biggest

11

YOU'RE THE PROBLEM

Sometimes, you yourself may unwittingly be the problem. Perhaps one of your team applied for the job you've just got, and resents you for displacing them. It never hurts to ask your boss about this as a matter of course: 'Did any of my team apply for this job?' That way, you're prepared. If ther's no problem, it's probably best not to mention to the team member that you know they were turned down in favour of you.

But if you do encounter this kind of trouble, talk to the person concerned frankly. Tell them you are aware that they too applied for the job, and you appreciate they are in a difficult position. Point out that you need them on your side, because they are clearly one of the most experienced and valuable people on your team.

customer is going under. This is information you need to know about fast. It's likely that if you keep your ears and eyes open, you'll catch a whiff of something wrong pretty early on. People will drop hints: 'Our next big launch won't be until next year now (if we're still here).'

Make sure you pick people up on any comments like this, with an innocent 'What do you mean?' Sooner or later, someone will tell you what they mean. If you think there's trouble but no one's

If the despatch department are traditionally at loggerheads with your department, you want to know about it sooner rather than later

talking openly to you, socialize with your colleagues and do more listening than talking. Once they all but forget you're there, they'll start to talk more freely.

Dishonest business practice

From share dealing to operating a racist selection procedure, illegal dumping to cheating on overtime, there is never any excuse for getting involved in dishonest behaviour. Often, you may be personally liable even if you are only carrying out company policy set by someone else. If you suspect that there are dishonest dealings in your organization, don't jump to conclusions. But do ask questions to make sure nothing you are being asked to do is dishonest or illegal. An innocent question can often set your mind at rest: 'Where do we dump our toxic waste?' If you are still unsure, don't bury your head in the sand: make sure you find out what the score is.

If you discover that dishonest practices are going on around you, you will have to make your own decision on how that affects your position ethically. From a legal point of view, you may want to take professional advice.

for later...

Your new organization is full of people who know more than you do about your department and even your job. So keep your ears open for clues, and take any opportunity to find out more about the history of your department. And bear in mind that it is the skeletons that will be hardest to drag out of the closet – it's not the good news that you'll have trouble eliciting from people.

Go for lunch or a drink after work with a couple of your colleagues who run other departments. They will often be the readiest to talk about past problems and successes – it's no skin off their nose to tell you that your predecessor was hugely popular with the team, for example, while your team members themselves might be too polite to ram it down your throat that you have a hard act to follow.

If you suspect that there are dishonest dealings in your organization, don't jump to conclusions. But do ask questions

5 the people

This chapter may not have come first, but don't let that fool you. Getting to know your team is the most important part of your new job, followed by getting to know everyone else you will be working with closely. (You'll find a page at the back of the book for making notes on who you need to talk to.) As a manager, you are only as good as your team, and they are only as good as their manager. So you are mutually dependent.

If you could wave a magic wand, you would meet with your boss, study your paperwork and get to know your team simultaneously. Without a magic wand, you have to do them in sequence, and meeting the boss and researching the files have to come first because they inform your meetings with your team members. But be aware that if it didn't have to happen this way round, talking to the team would be your top priority.

Your team members are not going to be impressed with a new boss who turns up, says hello briefly, and then disappears into the secrecy of their office for a whole morning. So although you may have to cover some other ground before you talk to your team formally, find time to talk to them informally in between. Take a couple of coffee breaks and chat to them about work or anything else, just to get to know each other.

PREPARE THE GROUND

Your new team members may be understandably nervous if you summon them to your office, so warn them in advance what to expect. Call them together if you can – maybe over a cup of coffee – and explain that you will be talking to each of them individually. Tell them that this is largely for your own benefit: you're hoping that they will be able to tell you what you need to know to do the job. You're not going to be reviewing their performance, so there's nothing to worry about.

thinking smart

RULE OF THUMB

Aim to start your individual sessions with your team members straight after lunch on your first day (or sooner if you can manage it). But during the morning, make sure you speak to everyone a couple of times at least – after the intial introductions – over coffee or just wandering around for a chat. So, by the time you see them individually they already feel they're getting to know you.

Take this opportunity to set the pattern by letting them know that from what you've gathered so far, you're lucky enough to have a good team behind you and you're looking forward to working with them. This will help them relax and recognize that they are in for a pleasant, friendly chat with you, rather than a formal, uncomfortable meeting.

To this end, you also need to make sure that you establish the right atmosphere in your office (or wherever you will be meeting them). Don't sit across a desk from them: this simply sets up a barrier between the two of you. Ideally, you should sit well away from a desk in easy chairs around a coffee table – and with a cup of coffee or tea each. Borrow a meeting room if you need to. If you really can't get away from the desk, sit at the side of it – at right angles to them – so that you are not in a dominant position. And make sure your chair is similar to theirs. No luxury swivel leather armchair while they sit on a hard plastic upright chair.

INDIVIDUAL SESSIONS

So now you've got your team members in front of you, one by one, what are you going to do with them? It's very simple, actually. You're going to ask them questions. Lots of them.

These people have most of the information you want to do your job well. So you need to get it out of them. This is no time to start telling them what you're going to do, or what you expect of them – you can't make those decisions until you have prised the information out of them. You're not asking them how to do your job – that's for you to decide. You're just asking them what you need to know.

And boy, is there a lot they can tell you. From why you're over budget to who gets on with whom, from what's gone wrong with a key account

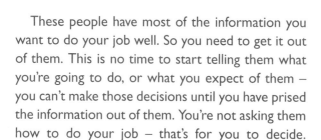

thinking smart

SHOW YOUR APPROVAL

You want to encourage your team members to spill the beans. Some information you're asking for is totally inocuous, but you might also want information that they might feel uncomfortable about giving you. Perhaps it makes them feel disloyal to your predecessor, or to one of their colleagues. Or maybe they are worried they will come across as inefficient or picky.

You can't make people break confidences or give you information they don't want to. So give them plenty of encouragement and approval, and absolutely no disapproval. If information is sensitive or difficult in any way, thank them for passing it on to you, and let them know it will help you do your job better.

to why morale is low. Someone, perhaps everyone, on your team can fill in most of the blanks for you if you just ask the right questions. And they can all tell you about themselves too: whether their performance is as good as it could be, whether they are being stretched, whether they enjoy working in the team.

So what questions should you ask? You're best off relaxing them by asking them questions about themselves, before you move on to questions about the team and the organization (which might call on them to make criticisms they are uneasy making). You may well know what you want to ask, so take the following lists as a guide rather than gospel.

Questions about themselves

- ▶ **What is your job, and what is its purpose?**
- ▶ **What systems and people do you rely on to do your job well?**
- ▶ **How could you do your job better?**
- ▶ **Which parts of your job do you enjoy most?**
- ▶ **Do you feel you are stretched to the full?**

Your precise choice of questions will also be influenced, of course, by your study of each team

member's personnel file, which will give you plenty
of clues as to their strengths and weaknesses,
problems and achievements.

Wider questions

▶ **What do you consider this team's greatest strengths to
be?**

▶ **And its weak points?**

▶ **How would you describe the morale of the team?**

▶ **Do you feel the team is achieving the best performance it
could?**

thinking smart

SCHEDULING THE INTERVIEWS

You're working to a tight schedule here, but ideally you
want to spend about 15 to 30 minutes with each team
member. If you're coming into a troubled department, you
might need even longer, especially with the more senior
members of your team. Try to fit in all the interviews
before the end of day two if you can – otherwise the people
at the end of the queue will start to feel unimportant.

Give yourself breaks between every two or three
interviews to catch up on anything else that needs doing, or
perhaps to carry out more research into topics that your
team members are raising.

You're best off asking them questions about themselves, before you move on to questions about the team and the organization

- ▶ **If you were in my position, what would you do to imporove the morale/performance of the team?**

- ▶ **How do you feel this team fits into the organization as a whole?**

- ▶ **What do you think are the greatest challenges facing this team at the moment?**

On top of this, you will also want to ask more specific questions, such as those we looked at in the last chapter arising from your study of the files and paperwork. This might include questions about the budget (particularly with senior team members), key projects and customer/supplier relationships.

You won't ask every team member exactly the same questions. And you will probably want to go into more depth with the most senior members of your team. If there is a dominant concern – such as

 thinking smart

BRIEF NOTES
You'll need to take notes during your team interviews, and this will show that you consider your team's views important. However, don't spend the whole time with your head buried in your notebook. Jot things down as briefly as possible – flesh them out later if you need to – so you can give most of your attention to the team member in person.

a failing relationship with a major customer – you may want to go into this thoroughly with the people who are involved most closely.

But you will need to ask each person something about themselves and something about wider issues. Not only are you informing yourself – you're also reassuring them that you're listening to their views. They may have been waiting months for a boss who might finally do something about the excessive workload in the department, or about the need to upgrade vital equipment. So let them see that you want to know what they consider priorities.

GROUP SESSIONS

Your first priority is to talk to your team members individually, for several reasons:

- (▶) **It gives you an in-depth view of them and of any problems they have.**

- (▶) **They may talk more freely when they are alone with you, especially about issues such as internal team difficulties.**

- (▶) **It helps you get to know them individually.**

- (▶) **It shows that you are interested in listening to each one of them.**

You will learn which issues concern all of them, and which are only raised by one or two of them. If you

You will probably want to go into more depth with the most senior members of your team put them all together, one will raise an issue, the rest will join in the discussion, and you'll have no clear idea how much importance they each attach to it.

However, you will also gain a huge amount by listening to them talking together. You will get a quick feel for a subject, and learn fast what are the most important decisions or concerns around it. Once they get their teeth into a debate, they will begin to forget you are there, so they will talk much more freely than they might one to one with you.

And you'll learn something else, too. If you watch and listen, you'll find out a great deal about the personalities and relationships within your new team. A debate about problems will show you:

- who is naturally respected by the rest of the team
- who are the natural leaders within the team
- who is less popular or less well respected
- any rivalries or factions within the team
- any person or group that tends to take a negative view
- your team's collective ability to analyze situations and solve problems

… you get the picture. A group session to discuss an important issue will tell you far more than your team realize.

HOT TOPICS

You're under time pressure here, and you can't possibly hope to find time to discuss every important issue in a group session. So pick your top four to six topics, and aim to hold two or three sessions within the first week. The most burning issue may get a session all to itself, but otherwise try to fit in two topics per session – related ones, ideally (but when are things ever ideal?).

It should be perfectly obvious by day two – if you're following this book – what your key issues are. It may be the team's main project, or an obvious and major problem such as falling standards or a huge work backlog. If it isn't obvious, it shouldn't be on the list for discussion at this stage.

Arranging the sessions

So how about the practicalities? What sort of group sessions should you hold? When? And how? You want a situation formal enough for people to feel it is a proper meeting and they must stick to the subject, but relaxed enough for them to say freely what they think. The perfect situation is a working lunch, either in a company dining room or meeting room, or else at a nearby restaurant. Opt for whichever of these seems to fit the company culture

If you watch and listen, you'll find out a great deal about the personalities and relationships within your new team

best. Failing that, organize a session in a meeting room, preferably where you can all sit round on comfortable chairs without a desk between you. Make sure everyone has a cup of coffee or a cold drink and can relax as much as possible.

You want to have completed your individual sessions before you launch into your group sessions. Failing that – if the individual sessions are going to take a long time to get through – hold your first group session before any of the individual sessions. The point is that everyone is then on an equal footing, both in their own minds and in your perception of them. From their point of view, people may feel at a disadvantage if others have met you one to one but they haven't. And from your perspective, you may prejudge some team members on the basis of their group performance, while others will have been fresh when you met them face to face.

thinking smart

FULL HOUSE

You may have to be firm with your team about recognizing that they need to attend these group sessions. They are not optional, and you want everyone there. You won't get a proper feel for the dynamics of the team if some of its members are absent.

You want to kick off these sessions as soon as you can, because you urgently need to hear what the team has to say about the most important issues and problems you're going to encounter in your new department. So, when should you start your group sessions?

- ▶ **The top time to hold your first group session is at lunchtime on day two, having completed all your individual meetings by then.**

- ▶ **If your individual meetings are going to go on beyond lunchtime on day two, hold it at lunchtime on day one before you start your individual meetings.**

- ▶ **If you can't complete the individual meetings by the middle of day two, and it's impossible to arrange a session on your first day, schedule your first group session for lunchtime on day three.**

Aim to have two or three sessions in all over the course of your first week or week and a half – it depends partly on how soon you need to collect all the information. If there are any really pressing issues, you won't be able to wait more than a couple of days before filling yourself in on the background in this way. But don't wear your team out with three working lunches in a row – give them a lunchtime off between group sessions.

A working lunch will generally take an hour or so, so you should be able to discuss one or two topics in this time. If the lunch goes on longer, don't add more topics – have some social time at the end of the lunch instead. It's not fair on your team to wear them out too much over lunch, and it's not an example you want to set.

Running the sessions

Your role in running these sessions is a delicate one. You want to stay in the background as much as possible so that people will talk openly, but you also want to guide the discussion the way you want it to go. The way to achieve both of these aims is by asking questions. You will come across as someone who wants information, rather than

thinking smart

KEEP IT IN RESERVE

As time goes on, you are less likely to have any need for this kind of session. But if an old problem from before your time ever flares up, remember the option of calling a working lunch to get your team to fill you in on the background and come up with some useful ideas.

someone about to start making snap decisions or issuing orders. And you can stay far more in the background as you direct the debate.

You'll need to start by introducing the topic briefly, saying why you want to know about it, and asking an initial question or two. You might say, for example, 'I've called this session because it's becoming clear from talking to you all individually that the biggest challenge facing this department at the moment is clearing the huge backlog of work. I'd really appreciate you filling me in on the background to this, and giving me some of your ideas on how to tackle it. How did the backlog build up in the first place?'

Now you can largely sit back, and simply prompt where necessary. If everyone clams up to start with, pick someone to kick off. Choose someone who isn't too shy, and who has a particular understanding of the issue (you see why you want to have held the individual sessions first if you can): 'Meg, you've been here longer than anyone, I believe. How did the backlog start to build up?'

You presumably know what questions you want to ask, but they will always include questions along the line of:

- ▶ **What's the history of this issue?**
- ▶ **Why is it causing such a problem?**
- ▶ **What can we do about it?**

You need to sit back and listen, without throwing in any comments. If you can see an option the rest of the team aren't raising, phrase it as a question: 'What would happen if we simply outsourced the backlog and started afresh?'

As well as asking the questions you want answers to, you also need to ask questions to steer the discussion if:

- ▶ **It is starting to go round in circles.**
- ▶ **The team are digressing.**
- ▶ **Things start to get personal (now is not the time to start allocating blame or making accusations).**

If any of these start to happen, stamp on them fast (and imperceptibly) by simply using a question to change the subject slightly.

At the end of the session, thank the team very much for filling you in on the issue. Tell them their ideas are appreciated and you will be taking them seriously, but don't announce any snap decisions about precisely how you will deal with the problem.

TAKE TIME OUT

You don't want an all-out row if an issue turns out to be more controversial than you realized. But if the discussion does become a little heated, it can help to slot in some social time for everyone to cool down at the end.

MEETING THE REST OF THE CROWD

Your team are the most important people of all, and you've already met your boss, of course. But there are still plenty of other people it will help to talk to as early in the proceedings as possible, especially the managers of other departments you're going to be working closely with.

An informal chat with these people is your best bet, and talk to them individually as they are more likely to be indiscreet that way – or at least not to bother so much with diplomacy – which will work in your favour. You want them to tell you, among other things, who is a pain to work with, where the system is failing, and what type of proposals the MD always blocks. This sort of information is far more likely to come out in private than in front of other colleagues.

If you can see an option the rest of the team aren't raising, phrase it as a question

Some colleagues will be discreet even in private, but they may still give you valuable hints. In any case, they can also give you plenty of other non-sensitive but highly useful information. If there are one or two colleagues you expect to spend a lot of working time with, ask them out for a drink after work. You haven't got time to do this with everyone, however, so ask the others for half an

WORKING LUNCH

Use your lunchtimes wisely for the first week or two. Unless the company culture is weighted very heavily towards working through every lunchtime, it's far better to be seen to take your lunch breaks. It makes you look more relaxed and in control, and sets a good example to your staff – you're not a slave-driver or a workaholic, and they don't have to feel guilty for taking their lunch breaks.

At the same time, the working lunch is one of those great institutions that create an atmosphere of relaxed, informal business that's hard to duplicate any other way. So don't waste your lunch breaks either.

The answer is to take time for a pleasant, relaxed lunch, but always in the company of someone you can talk to about work ... and do a bit of socializing too. Hold group sessions or go for a drink with a colleague or even your boss; that way you can work and relax at the same time.

hour of their time over coffee or even a quick lunch. Half an hour isn't too much of their time, but it does give you a relaxed chance to go through a few questions and get to know them at the same time. You could get through the questions in ten or 15 minutes, but it would be more of a cross-examination than a getting-to-know-you session.

So what questions are you going to ask your colleagues? Obviously it depends partly on the working relationship you expect to have, but here is a guide:

- ▶ **In what areas do your team and mine work most closely?**
- ▶ **How has the relationship between the two departments been in the past?**
- ▶ **What do you see as the greatest challenges I'll encounter running my team?**
- ▶ **Are there any problems I'm going to meet that I ought to know about?**
- ▶ **If you were in my position, what would you consider your priorities for my department?**

In addition to this type of question, you might also have questions thrown up by your research into projects and your departmental history and so on.

Obviously, the job of getting to know people is an ongoing one, and you may well want to pick the

If there are one or two colleagues you expect to spend a lot of working time with, ask them out for a drink after work

brains of your boss, your colleagues or your team for some time to come. But this series of initial interviews and sessions should give you the fastest possible route to filling in as much background to your job as possible in a very short time. By the end of your first couple of days, you'll be feeling pretty well on top of things, and by the end of the first week you'll be raring to go.

for later...

Once you've been in the job for about a week or two, it's time to set targets for each member of your team. You can't do this immediately, since you don't know enough about what needs doing or what they are capable of. But just as you needed to ask your boss what your objective was and what was expected of you, so each of your team members needs to know what you expect of them.

It may well be that your team members already have targets they are working to, set by their previous boss. If so, you will still need to review these (although you may decide to leave them as they are).

Call in each team member individually and discuss their targets with them. No one is going to meet a target that is unrealistic, and they are not likely to meet one they are unhappy about. So, the process is not a matter of you saying; 'Right, I want a 5 per cent increase in sales from you in the next quarter,' or 'I expect complaints from internal customers to halve by the end of the year.'

Discuss what they are achieving now, and how much more they could achieve. A target should be attainable, but should stretch the team member. Well motivated people like to be stretched, so you won't have any trouble getting them to agree to a realistic target if you've been doing your job well for the last week or two. They will want to give their best if you have inspired them.

6 the outline plan

By the time you've worked your way through the first five chapters of this book, you should be two or three days into your new job. But with fast thinking and smart action, you should already have established:

- your objective
- what is expected of you
- what strengths you have been hired for (why you got the job)
- your resources and authority.

You will by now have met and talked in depth with:

- your boss
- your predecessor
- your team members
- your close colleagues.

And you will have identified:

- **your key projects**
- **any major challenges or problems facing your department**
- **your budget position**

... and with any luck you'll have picked up at least a few hints about any skeletons that may be lurking in the company closet.

Good. That's enough information – packed into a very short time – to enable you to assess your ability to do the job. And that's the next step. Your career depends heavily on making your mark in this job, so it's time to assess how easy it's going to be.

THREATS AND OPPORTUNITIES

The starting point for this process is to identify the threats and the opportunites that face you in running this department successfully. So let's begin with the threats. List the most striking problems you can see are going to occupy your time for the next few weeks or months. (You'll find a page at the back of the book to do just that.) There's no point giving yourself an unmanageable list of 50 or 60 problems; just concentrate on the key ones – those that are going to get in the way of meeting your objective unless you resolve them.

Even when you encounter massive problems in a new job, that doesn't have to mean that there are a lot of them. You might have just one overriding problem. There's really no mileage in having a list of more than four or five threats: you haven't the resources to tackle more than that at one go. Once they're dealt with, you can move on to the next raft of problems.

Every job will obviously have a different list of key threats, but here's an idea of the kind of things that might appear on yours. You'll notice that the nature of the threats can vary widely:

- ▶ **work backlog**
- ▶ **failing contract with key customer**
- ▶ **major budget overspend**
- ▶ **bad relationship with production department**
- ▶ **plans for next month's big launch in disarray**
- ▶ **damaging rivalry between team members**
- ▶ **huge overtime bill**
- ▶ **serious software problems that are hampering work**
- ▶ **planned redundancies on the team.**

So that's the kind of threat you need to have on your list of key issues to tackle as soon as possible. Now it's time for more cheerful matters: the opportunities. You are in a position to score some successes for your department, but you need to decide what they are going to be. Again, you want to draw up a list of key opportunities that will help to further your objective. These are the projects that are central to your success.

Once again, you're looking for a list of up to four or five for the time being – once they're under way, you can move on to the next batch. Everyone's list is different, but this sample will give you an idea:

thinking smart

SPOT THE DIFFERENCE

What's the difference between a threat and an opportunity? Suppose you list 'huge overtime bill' under threats. Why not list 'slash overtime bill' under opportunities instead? Can't you look at most threats as opportunities?

Yes, you can if you're into positive thinking; it's a great attitude to adopt. But there is a difference. If you're not sure which category to put any issue into, ask yourself this question: 'What happens if I do nothing?' If the result of inaction would be damaging to the department or the organization, then you are dealing with a threat. If the result would be no change at all – and the current situation isn't damaging – you have an opportunity on your hands.

Another way to look at it is that a threat demands a red light: it must be stopped. An opportunity needs a green light to make it go.

There's really no mileage in having a list of more than four or five threats: you haven't the resources to tackle more than that at one go

- (▶) **Increase market share by 3 per cent.**
- (▶) **Improve productivity by 5 per cent.**
- (▶) **Plan major showcase for new products for next year.**
- (▶) **Train more staff to operate new software to increase efficiency.**
- (▶) **Reduce complaints.**
- (▶) **Cut overtime bill.**
- (▶) **Increase positive coverage in national and trade press.**

These are the successes you can start planning to notch up over the next few weeks and months in the job.

STRENGTHS AND WEAKNESSES

So, are you up to the job? Now you know what the key threats and opportunities are, do you have what it takes to meet them successfully? Each one is going to need a different set of skills, and the only way to be sure you can meet the challenge in each case is to list the skills you need. Here are a few examples:

Threat: Failing contract with key customer.
Skills: Negotiating, selling.

Threat: Overtime bill.
Skills: Financial, diplomatic, organizational, decision-making.

Opportunity: Train more staff to operate new software.
Skills: Training, IT skills, planning.

Opportunity: Increase positive press coverage.
Skills: PR, writing, event-planning.

As a professional manager, you should know what your strengths and weaknesses are. You need to go through your lists honestly, and identify the threats and opportunities that you are well equipped to tackle, and those that you may be weak in. Some managers are tempted to duck issues that they know they are going to be weak at handling, but smart managers address the weaknesses and develop the skills. If a threat is there, it must be met. And a good opportunity should never be missed just because you're not sure you're up to it.

Handling weaknesses

So what do you do if a threat or opportunity calls for a skill you don't have? There are three solutions you can apply (you may choose to apply more than one):

▶ **Go and train yourself.** Enrol on an evening course, buy a good book on the subject, find an online training programme, ask a friend or colleague who is an expert to teach you.

▶ **Ask for training.** Talk to your boss. Explain that you feel you are weak in an area that is going to be important, and that you would like to be given training to help you do your job better.

▶ **What's your team for?** As a manager, you can't delegate discipline interviews or drawing up budgets. But if you have a top-notch negotiator on your team, or someone with a gift for organizing events, use them. It's what they're there for. What matters is that the team as a whole has the strengths to meet the threat or the opportunity – not necessarily that you personally have them.

thinking smart

SKILLS TRAINING

You may not want to admit to your boss – especially at this early stage – that you're not great at handling people or organizing events. These are skills it might be better to work on privately or to delegate where you can. But where you lack practical skills, you should certainly say so. If this is your first job as a manager, you may never have had to draw up a budget before. For some jobs, you need to learn to use a new piece of software. Or maybe you need training in how to conduct selection interviews. So ask your boss to arrange for you to have the training you need.

OUTLINE PLANS

You have your two lists of key issues to tackle: threats and opportunities. You've identified any weaknesses that may hamper your chances of success, and you're doing something about them. So now you need to draw up an outline plan for each issue on your list, so that you know how you're going to tackle it and in what kind of timeframe.

For example, let's take the threat that the plans for next month's launch are in disarray. You might decide that the only way to get them back on track is to:

▶ **Go through the plans with key team members in the next 48 hours and simplify them.**

▶ **Get all press and customer invitations out by the end of next week.**

▶ **Call in an outside event organizer to pull the rest of the plans together on time.**

Having drawn up your outline plan, you need to check what resources you need to carry them out. Do you have the resources and the authority? Can you bring in an outside event organizer off your own bat? And have you got the money to do it? Do you have the staff available to attend the launch, or will you have to find people from elsewhere?

COVER YOURSELF

Sometimes, you can see that something that is expected of you simply isn't possible. Maybe there is no way next month's launch can possibly succeed at such short notice without spending money that you don't have in your budget. Perhaps the backlog can't be cleared without cooperation from another department, which isn't forthcoming.

Talk to your boss and ask for the resources you need. If you get no joy, put your case in writing, stating that you cannot achieve what is expected of you without the additional resources. Then at least you're covered if there's any comeback later.

For each of your key threats and opportunities, you need to draw up an outline plan and then list any resources you will need for it, or identify any areas where you need authorization from higher up the organization. This process shouldn't take too long, particularly since your lists shouldn't run to more than about eight threats or opportunities between them.

Once you have completed this outline planning, you're ready to sink your teeth into your new job. You've met the people, you've covered the background, and now you know where you're going. So off you go. Good luck!

for later...

Once you have your outline plans drawn up, you're ready to get cracking with the job. It is essential that you don't allow yourself to get so bogged down in everyday work that these key plans start to slip. You have already specified a timeframe for each one: mark key stages in your diary and make sure they happen.

Starting with the most urgent, work through each of these outline plans and flesh out the detail. You will probably want to bring in at least some of your team members to help you do this. Once the plans are worked out, you can start delegating tasks and getting things moving.

As soon as you begin to work through these threats and opportunities, add more on to the end of the list to replace those you have dealt with. This way you will always have about half a dozen or so core projects central to your objective under way at any time to keep your department moving towards its goals, and to keep you notching up fresh successes.

flying start in half a day

What if you're starting work on the day of some major event? You arrive at 9.30 in the morning, and by 2.00 in the afternoon you're expected to be shaking hands with customers or attending a conference. You've got half a day to get in, get settled, and get to know everyone. It's tough, but you can do it.

I hope you're reading this book before the morning you start work, so you should have time to read the whole thing comfortably. Here are a few guidelines for compressing its contents into half a day:

- ▶ **If it's not too late, call your soon-to-be boss and ask for all the background material on the organization you can get hold of (corporate newsletters, annual reports, press releases etc.), including copies of your departmental budget and any key documents from project files.**

- ▶ Get in touch with your predecessor – who may still be in post – and pick their brains for all the information you can get (see Chapter 4).

- ▶ It's tempting when time is tight to allow yourself to be rushed through the introductions. But since they may be your only chance this morning to talk to people, you should set a slower pace than you otherwise might so you can really imprint the key team members and colleagues on your memory.

- ▶ First impressions are vitally important whether you have half a day or half a year to settle in, so make sure that you appear relaxed and calm as far as possible, and follow the guidelines in Chapter 2.

- ▶ You'll still need to hold your meeting with your boss first thing; set this up before the day you start work if you can.

- ▶ Go through the files as outlined in Chapter 4, but give them just a cursory skim for the time being – you're simply looking for glaring problems or issues for now. Find a chance to go through the paperwork in more detail as soon as you can.

- ▶ You won't be able to hold individual meetings with each of your team members today – but schedule them in as soon as you can. However, try to fit in the first group session today, over lunch if possible, or else over coffee. It will give you and your team a feel for each other, and you'll start to get a valuable sense of the key issues and the company culture.

flying start in an hour

Wheeee! You're not hitting the ground running, you're hitting the ground from 30 000 feet without a parachute. They really have landed you in it, haven't they? Turn up at 9.00 and be stuck into the job by 10.00? Any organization that kicks off at that speed isn't going to slow down later; you can expect to do a lot of fast thinking between now and your next career move.

So what can you realistically achieve in an hour? A lot less than you can manage in two to three days, obviously. But all the work in this book is essential, so you're going to have to make sure it gets fitted in somehow, and within the next week or so at the most. But for now:

1 Call your boss a few days before you start (if it's not too late already) and ask for all the background information on the organization they can send you, and copies of any important

files (see Chapter 4) that they are prepared to let you have.

2 Make an appointment for a 15- to 20-minute meeting with your boss to start half an hour after you arrive on your first day.

3 Get hold of your predecessor and pick their brains (see Chapter 4).

4 Turn up early. It may not be much, but it will help.

5 f you are early enough, and you can find them, spend this extra time looking through the files on major projects.

6 Spend your first (official) half hour meeting your team and talking to them (see Chapter 1). Decline any introductions outside your team for now, along with any guided tours, unless they seem essential. Remember the guidelines in Chapter 2 on making a good impression.

7 Spend the next quarter of an hour or so with your boss, getting answers to the questions outlined in Chapter 3.

8 Use your remaining time to have a quick look through the personnel files before you get thrown in at the deep end.

 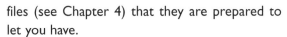

An hour isn't long, but this way you have time to cover a little of everything so at least you gain breadth of knowledge, if not depth. Although there are other essential areas to cover – such as meetings with your team – you can fit these in over the next few days. And bear in mind that you will arguably bond with people, and absorb the company culture, faster this way than if you had longer to find your feet.

You have time to cover a little of everything so you gain breadth of knowledge, if not depth

key people

U se this page to list the key people you need to talk to in your first week. Tick them off as you meet each one so that you can make sure you miss no one out. Remember to include:

- ▶ **Your immediate boss**
- ▶ **Your predecessor**
- ▶ **All your team members**
- ▶ **Fellow managers of other departments**
- ▶ **Any other colleagues or ex-employees of the organisation who may be helpful.**

key issues
and projects

Note down here the top issues and projects you need to get on top of in your first few days. You can also jot down any questions about them which you want to ask the people you talk to over the next few days.

threats

You need to keep a constant eye on the key threats facing your department, and give priority to addressing them. Note down here what they are so you can hold a quick mental review of them over the next few weeks.

opportunities

Missed opportunities are missed successes for your organisation, your department, and yourself personally. To make sure you can't miss any key opportunities, write them down here and then review them regularly to check you are making good progress on each.